Little Books of Guidance
Finding answers to life's big questions!

Also in the series:
What Is Christianity? by Rowan Williams
Who Was Jesus? by James D. G. Dunn
How Can Anyone Read the Bible? by L. William
    Countryman
What Happens When We Die? by Thomas G. Long
What About Sex? by Tobias Stanislas Haller, BSG

WHY GO TO CHURCH?

A Little Book of Guidance

C. K. ROBERTSON

Church Publishing
NEW YORK

Unless otherwise noted, the Scripture quotations contained herein are from the New Revised Standard Version Bible, copyright © 1989 by the Division of Christian Education of the National Council of Churches of Christ in the U.S.A. Used by permission. All rights reserved.

Church Publishing
19 East 34th Street
New York, NY 10016
www.churchpublishing.org

Cover design by Jennifer Kopec, 2Pug Design
Typeset by Progressive Publishing Services

Library of Congress Cataloging-in-Publication Data

A record of this book is available from the Library of Congress.

ISBN-13: 978-0-89869-119-1 (pbk.)
ISBN-13: 978-0-89869-263-1 (ebook)

Printed in the United States of America

Contents

Room for One More

"Why go to church?" The fortysomething businessman sitting next to me on the plane had just asked what I do for a living, the usual small talk as we prepared for takeoff. Putting my book down, I smiled and told him that I was a priest. His matter of fact response was the question above. It's a fair question. I decided to counter with my own: "Why *not* go to church?" Suddenly my acquaintance turned sheepish and looked down: "I went with my family when I was a kid, but I really don't have time now. And I figure I can pray wherever I am." Then, straightening up, he looked me straight in the eye, and with a smirk he added a more direct comment: "Anyway, there are a lot of hypocrites in churches."

My reply was immediate, "Too true, but the good news is that there's always room for one more." He paused and then burst out laughing. "Good answer," he said, his hand outstretched and his smile bigger than ever, "okay, so tell me why I should consider going to church." Returning his smile and shaking his hand, I put my book away for the duration of the flight as we enjoyed an honest, heartfelt conversation.

In times past, that businessman's question might have appeared nonsensical. Of course you went to church! Indeed, this remains true today in many places across the globe and, yes, even in some parts of this country. However, the fact is that the man on the plane represents a significant number of people in the United States who do not attend church. While there have been other periods in modern history when numbers have decreased (the turbulent 1960s come to mind), the exodus in more recent years has been significant enough that some speak of the Great Decline.

Even in the southern United States, the so-called Bible Belt, where a significant majority of people claim that religion is very important in their lives, regular attendance at worship still barely hovers around 50 percent. And in New England and the Pacific Northwest, areas generally acknowledged as the least religious in the nation, only one out of five adults regularly attend services. These "nones," as they have come to be termed, are a growing group.

Their reasons for non-attendance vary but usually fall under several familiar themes. Some simply don't believe in God or experienced some crisis of faith. Others dislike what they call "organized religion," often citing the hypocrisy of members (like my seatmate on the plane), the undue focus on politics, or internal conflicts. Still others speak vaguely of being "spiritual but not religious," or they proffer that they are quite simply too busy to add one more commitment to their weekly calendar. Throughout the country, it is common on a Sunday morning to find more people in line at the local coffee shop than in the pews of the local church.

But there remain many who find themselves drawn to, or perhaps drawn back to, a place that offers not only coffee but other more intangible goods, such as an experience that satisfies a longing of the soul. In the tenth century, a Russian prince sent representatives to the famed Church of Holy Wisdom in Constantinople. The report they gave upon their return to Kiev still strikes a chord: "We don't know whether we were in heaven or earth . . . we only know that God dwells there among people." Their glowing recommendation was met with open ears and an open heart, as that medieval leader discovered something very special.

"Why go to church?" The question remains today one well worth answering, whether by individuals who want to take a look for themselves or by congregations who seek to better welcome these "spiritual shoppers." Whichever group you find yourself in, the following pages offer practical answers to practical questions. For clarity's sake, this small book of guidance is sub-divided into three parts.

Chapter 1 tackles the question, "What's the point of church anyway?" This section explores a few key reasons for seriously considering regular involvement in a community of faith and worship that, while imperfect, can be a great gift in your life.

Chapter 2 goes on to address, "How do I choose a church?" and presents the various factors to consider when looking for a place to call your spiritual home. This section is also helpful for congregational members who want to find ways to be more intentional and effective in greeting and welcoming newcomers.

Chapter 3 caps it off by addressing the query, "What do I do when I'm there?" This looks at everything from when to sit, stand, and kneel during the service to how to become involved and move from first-time visitor to fully integrated member.

Following a brief conclusion, you will find an appendix, listing other books and resources that can prove invaluable for further exploration, as well as a glossary of key terms, which can help when you hear some indecipherable church-talk!

There are many different brands of churches out there, each with their own strengths and weaknesses. This book is about churches in the Episcopal branch of the Jesus Movement, a tradition that is known for both its rich heritage and its unapologetic commitment to inclusion of all as a gospel imperative. In the Book of Common Prayer (BCP), in the service called, "The Consecration of a Church," there is a wonderful description of a church as a place where we are "made one with Christ and with one another." It is a community that is well worth exploring.

As I recall my encounter on that plane years ago, and the conversation that grew out of a seemingly simple question, I give thanks to God for that forty-something businessman and so many other honest skeptics and faithful seekers like him, as well as for those who strive to welcome them with outstretched arms.

This book is for all of them. This book is for you.

What's the Point of Church Anyway?

"Let the doors be opened." (BCP, p. 568)

Mary didn't go to church when she was growing up. Her parents always said that she should be allowed to make up her own mind about religion, and they didn't want to force her into any one way. On Sunday mornings, she simply slept in.

Mary was always a bit curious though, especially when her friends would go to Midnight Mass on Christmas Eve, or talk about preparing for their confirmation. She visited one friend's Pentecostal church a couple times, attended another's bar mitzvah at the local synagogue, and went to a cousin's wedding in a Roman Catholic cathedral. That was, however, the extent of her young religious experience.

Somewhere deep inside, Mary felt like she was missing something.

She was just shy of thirty when a friend from work invited her to come for a special service at her Episcopal church. The occasion was her friend's commissioning as a lay reader. Mary didn't know exactly what that meant, but she agreed to go. That morning, as she looked and listened and took in all that was happening around her in the service, Mary somehow knew— whether it was logical or otherwise—that this was a place, a community, that she could call . . . home.

A Place of Belonging

"We receive you into the household of God." (BCP, p. 308)

Years ago, a popular television sitcom opened each episode with a catchy tune that spoke of a place "where everybody knows your name." The place in question was a local bar, the neighborhood watering hole, where week in and week out, viewers watched the cast regulars swap stories, laugh, argue, and connect. Who doesn't want a place like that?

When that show was running, I was living in a village in England, unique in some ways but not unlike countless other villages throughout the country. Village life invariably centers around two places where people come together, the local pub and the village church. My house was situated directly between the two. Yes, the pub was lively on evenings after work and weekends, but it was the church where people were connected on a deeper level, through baptisms, weddings, and funerals . . . the stuff of life. During the week, the church hosted a moms and toddlers program, recovery groups, youth activities, and small group studies.

Back here across the pond, twenty-first century America in many ways resembles the first-century Roman Empire. It is a complex system where an increasing number of people with diverse backgrounds and languages live side by side in urban and suburban areas, yet often they find themselves feeling disconnected and isolated.

Church can be a spiritual village for folks who want to connect in meaningful ways. The Episcopal Book of Common Prayer, in its service for the consecration of a church, includes a summary of what the church community can be: "Be with us as new members are added to your household, as we grow in grace through the years, when we are joined in marriage, when we turn to you in sickness or special need, and at the last, when we are committed into the Father's hands" (BCP, p. 569).

In first-century Rome, where people were segregated by ethnicity and race, gender, and class, the apostle Paul spoke of the church as God's "new creation," within which all the distinctions that kept people apart disappeared. In the "household of God," Paul declared, "there is neither Jew nor Greek, slave nor free, male and female, for all are one in Christ" (Gal. 3:28). In the centuries since Paul's time, churches at their worst have fallen into the patterns of the surrounding society, so in the mid-twentieth century, Dr. Martin Luther King, Jr. could rightly speak of 11a.m. on Sunday mornings as "the most segregated hour in America."

But the good news is that at their best, churches provide a kind of extended family where there is always room for one more, where unity does NOT equal uniformity, and where integration and inclusion can become the norm. It is not a coincidence that almost exactly in the middle of the service of Holy Eucharist, the principal weekly worship service in most parishes, there occurs the Peace, when the gathered people greet one another with handshakes and hugs. The message is clear: in church, strangers can become friends, and people of all sorts and conditions can recognize one another as brothers and sisters in Christ. They are ready to come to the communion table together, not because they are all the same, but because they are all beloved by God.

Make no mistake, there are still problems in churches, tensions and conflicts that arise. Because it is still a human institution, we would be naïve to paint the church in an overly romantic light. As Archbishop-emeritus Desmond Tutu once said, "the church is a messy but lovable family." It is appropriate, therefore, that the weekly service unapologetically includes readings and prayers that sometimes speak of sin. The goal is not to be depressing. It is rather to acknowledge the reality of the human condition, so that we can take seriously the call to strive—prayerfully, intentionally, and with God's help—for something better, to live "in unity, constancy, and peace" (p. 363), and "to do the work God has given us to do" (p. 366).

Remember Mary, who visited her friend's church? One of the key things that impressed her as she experienced that Eucharistic service was the feeling of community. The people around her in the congregation clearly liked being with each other, and their smiles were genuine when they looked her in the eyes and said, "God's peace be with you." She found, as have countless others, that church can be a place of belonging. That was one key reason she decided to return. Another reason was that in church, Mary, again like many others, discovered something profound, something awe-inspiring, and something that might best be described as holy.

An Encounter with the Holy

"Be always near us when we seek you in this place." (BCP, p. 568)

Church is not simply a social club or special interests group. It is focused on things spiritual, where you can feel the presence of God in a special way. For as long as we humans have walked on earth, we have marked certain places as sacred spaces. It is not about limiting the divine to a single spot. After all, God is the Creator of the universe! But churches and other religious sites are set apart precisely to remind us of that divine presence, which we can so easily miss in our everyday routine. Even people who have long counted themselves as agnostic can find themselves deeply touched upon walking into a great gothic cathedral or a quiet parish chapel.

It is more than just architectural beauty. Walk through the doors on Christmas Eve night, you take in the aroma of garlands and incense, you hear the voices of the choir and the chimes of the bells, you see the Altar bedecked in gold and white, and you taste the bread and wine. And as the service winds down and midnight marks the new day, you find yourself kneeling with everyone else, as the lights are turned off, and the darkness is broken only by the candles that all of you are holding, lighted in turn from person to person. Quiet reigns until you hear words from the beginning of John's Gospel read aloud: "In the beginning was the Word, and the Word was with God, and the Word was God . . . and the Word became flesh and lived among us." Then, still kneeling, you join the rest of the congregation in singing acapella the quiet, familiar hymn, "Silent Night." It is, without doubt, a magical night.

Or you enter a very different church on Epiphany, All Saints Sunday, or whenever, and you find chairs arranged in arced rows, instead of the pews you expected. Two great screens hang from the high ceiling, carefully situated so as not to obstruct the view of the large oaken Table up front and center. Off to the left a worship band of guitars, drums, and a keyboard lead a congregation of all ages in songs unfamiliar, but the tunes are easy to follow and the lyrics are projected on the screens. The priest preaches without notes, not from a pulpit, but walking along the dais. When she has finished, you join the congregation in renewing vows once made by your parents at your baptism, and then as the Peace is proclaimed, you are swept up in the crowd of smiles and hugs that seems to go on and on. You are swept up in the act of worship!

Whatever the specifics of the experience, church is where people go for more than good company; it is where they gather together to worship, learn, pray, and be blessed. There is variety enough out there to be able find a worship experience that fits your needs and desires (and we will talk more about this in a little bit). But the key thing is that church is one place—not the only place, of course, but a very special place—where you can share a spiritual experience, an encounter with the One who created you, the One who wants to touch you in a profound way even now.

And from this encounter, you can choose to expand your spiritual horizons, deepen your sense of purpose, and become more truly the person God has called you to be.

A Center for Personal Formation

"Blessed Lord, who caused all Holy Scripture to be written for our learning: Grant us so to hear them, read, mark, learn, and inwardly digest them." (BCP, p. 236)

Churches are places of worship, yes, but they are also training grounds, where participants are not only comforted but where they are challenged, and where they are not just fed but where they are formed. As a wise priest once told me, in church God welcomes you just as you are but loves you enough not to leave you there. Called by some a "school for sinners" and by others a "school for saints," church is both, because you and I are both, with sinfulness and saintliness all mixed together.

The worship service itself is an opportunity for learning and personal formation. Within the Eucharist, you hear readings from both the Old Testament and New Testament, followed by a sermon or reflection that helps make those readings become clearer and more relevant to you. The Nicene Creed follows, proclaimed in unison by the entirety of the congregation, a centuries-old summary of the Christian faith that we profess, and before we receive communion, we hear another summary of what Jesus did out of love for us in what is called the Eucharistic Prayer.

Beyond the service, most churches offer a menu of various learning opportunities. These often include children's Sunday school, of course, where the youngest attendees can hear Bible stories and important things about God in language that is understandable. Sometimes there are children's liturgies, or worship opportunities, that likewise are child-friendly while at the same time echoing the rhythm and patterns of the adult service, so as to prepare children for a fairly seamless transition into the "grownup service."

Beyond these Sunday offerings for children, many churches also offer a range of adult and youth pro-grams, sometimes on Sunday mornings between services and sometimes during the week, sometimes in the parish hall, and sometimes in people's homes. There are Holy Scripture studies, focusing on a particular book of the Bible, or book studies that can offer small groups the chance to discuss a classic volume on faith by someone like C. S. Lewis and Teresa of Avila, or a contemporary bestseller that has everyone talking. There are opportunities such as recovery programs, prayer circles, financial stewardship classes, Christian meditation trainings, inquirers classes, confirmation courses. One parish I served held a series of programs called Teaching Tuesdays. They would run for four weeks two or three times a year, and they were intended for people in the community as well as in the parish. Themes included parenting tools, issues of aging, and holistic wellness.

Now the beauty is that none of these learning opportunities are mandatory. No one is going to force you to attend anything if you don't want to do so. All the additional offerings that a church provides throughout the week are gifts that you can choose to unwrap for yourself or not. But the possibility for real growth as a person, as a beloved child of God, is there before you whenever you choose to make use of it.

A Community for Others

"Lord, make us instruments of your peace." (BCP, p. 833)

We are meant to do more than live only for ourselves. My kids have heard me say more times than I (or they) can count that the most important thing in life is to make a difference. It is something that was impressed on me in church. It starts within the church community itself, as we care for one another. Way back in the beginning of Christianity, the apostle Paul spoke of the followers of Jesus as the body of Christ, each part connected to the others: "If one part of the body suffers, they all suffer."

Years ago, I overheard a conversation between two members of a church. One was quite dejected, practically in despair as the result of numerous disappointments and difficulties at home. "I'm not sure I even believe any more," I heard him say. The other did not flinch but simply put his hand on his fellow parishioner's shoulder and quietly replied, "That's okay; we'll believe for you for now." When you are in a church, it is not simply that you belong but that you are able to be there for your fellow members and to make a difference in their lives.

But far more than this, church is where together you all can have a significant impact on the world around you. Recently, during a meeting with several federal lawmakers, I was reminded of the remarkable fact that churches comprise the largest health care distribution network on the continent of Africa, and probably in many other places around the globe. This is because of the presence of congregations on the ground in every town and village and in places that are otherwise off the grid for most governmental organizations and

NGOs. By utilizing these existing networks, your local parish can literally connect with people on the other side of the world.

And in our own neighborhoods, churches are some of the most effective providers of immediate assistance and care. Episcopalians often speak of the 25th chapter of the Gospel of Matthew as a charter for making the world a better place: feeding the hungry through food pantries and soup kitchens; visiting those who are homebound or in hospitals, nursing homes, and even prisons; and building homes for those who might never otherwise have enjoyed what you and I take for granted.

And besides what it means for others, these opportunities make a difference in our lives as well. I recall a woman in her seventies who, because of serious health issues, was homebound. So much of her life seemed to disappear when the four walls of her house became her entire world, but the church gave her new life and purpose. First, she suddenly learned firsthand what it means to be part of a parish family, as she became the recipient of regular visits by her fellow lay members, bringing communion to her, sharing stories, praying with her. But perhaps even more importantly, her priest asked her to start writing welcome letters to newcomers and sympathy cards for members going into the hospital. This woman became not only a recipient of care but also an important caregiver herself, with a vital ministry that kept her connected and allowed her to make a difference . . . despite her limitations.

So, what's the point of church anyway? Let's return to our friend Mary. She decided to go back to her colleague's church a couple of weeks after her first visit. She then returned a week after that. It wasn't long before it indeed became her spiritual home. In late February, she started attending a weekly Lenten home study group. The theme was different forms of prayer. She learned so much, but also felt as if there was so much more that she wanted to learn. So a few months later, when the priest started a set of inquirers classes for those who wanted to learn more about the church and what it means to be an Episcopal Christian, Mary enthusiastically signed up.

As the months passed, Mary's co-workers and friends remarked about the difference they noticed in her since she started attending church. It was all positive. As one friend said, she seemed more grounded, more at peace with herself. Far from disconnecting her from her old life, being part of the church somehow seemed to help Mary become even more engaged in her life and friendships. Yes, it was clear to everyone, including Mary herself, that this was a very good thing.

When someone asked Mary what the point of church was for her, she was quick to respond: "Church is where I have tapped into spiritual depths I didn't even know were there, and I am a stronger and more caring person because of it."

How Do I Choose a Church?

"Let us give thanks . . . for this place, where we may be still and know that you are God." (BCP, p. 578)

Churches are not all alike. Like individuals, churches have their own personalities, their unique histories, their idiosyncrasies, their own patterns and priorities. I should clarify that I am going to be talking here about different types of *Episcopal* churches, as that is our context here. But even under that umbrella, you will find quite a diverse range. People sometimes talk about "church shopping," and this is not a bad thing. It is important to see what works for you and to not be discouraged if you visit one and find that it is not a match for you. But where do you start?

Size Might Make a Difference

When high school seniors start looking at colleges, they usually give significant consideration to the size of the school. This makes sense, given there are different pros and cons to consider when choosing a large, medium, or small school. Even so, churches come in different sizes, each bringing with it issues of staffing, numbers of services and programs, and the relationship of church members with the clergy and lay leadership. They can be narrowed down into four basic categories. First, there are *family* churches, with several dozen members at most, where everyone basically knows all the other members, and where each member has a personal direct connection to the priest. Unless a *family* church is heavily endowed, the odds are that its budget is small, matching its membership numbers. There is, therefore, only enough money to pay for one priest and possibly a part-time parish administrator. In fact, many such churches have only part-time or even non-stipendiary clergy. This usually means that pastoral care, teaching programs, preaching and liturgy are the responsibility of the one person, who acts as a personal chaplain to all.

There are also *pastoral* churches, which range in numbers from several dozen to well over a hundred active parishioners. As in the previous category, churches of this size usually rely on a single key clergyperson, with whom the majority of the congregation most likely still feel a personal connection. But the greater numbers allow for a greater body of volunteers than in a *family* church, and the budget may allow for more part-time staff. The result can be more services, more programs, increased music possibilities, and a greater diversity in membership composition. Many Episcopal churches are *pastoral* congregations. The beauty of this size for many newcomers is that there is a sense of intimacy like the *family* sized church, but just enough numbers so that you can feel like there is room to be adopted in.

Next up are *program* churches. The name says it all. While the *pastoral* church is still in many ways pastor-focused, here programs are a draw. Larger numbers and a larger budget allow for a larger staff, which means that church members no longer necessarily feel a personal connection to the rector, or head priest. Here, there are probably other clergy, full and part-time, as well as committees or commissions that share the responsibilities of ministry and leadership. The result is a lot of energy and a lot of opportunities to be on both the giving and receiving ends of teaching, pastoral, and outreach programs. With people usually attending one of the multiple services on a weekend and during the week, you find different congregations all within the same church, almost like different neighborhoods or villages in a single big city. This can be appealing to a newcomer if you want to enter quietly, not get known too quickly, and sample some of the possibilities open to you.

Finally, there are *corporate* or *resource* parishes. These are far fewer in number, but you can find them in various geographical locales. Here the head priest is more CEO than personal pastor, overseeing a very large staff, perhaps with several full-time clergy and many lay employees, and a significant array of services and programs supported by a large budget. The churches are sometimes larger in both members and funds than some dioceses. Here you can be simply one among many, but at the same time such churches often provide outlets for personal connection, through home study groups or generational and special interest networks.

There is another group of churches in a category all its own: *cathedrals.* Whatever its size, a cathedral is unique insofar as it is the bishop's church, for there stands the bishop's chair, or *cathedra.* Some, like St. John the Divine in New York, Grace in San Francisco, and the National Cathedral in Washington, DC, are grand and historic, attracting tourists as much as worshippers. Most are far smaller, but still offer a different experience than a local parish church.

No matter what the size and composition of the church, they hold in common several crucial things: worship that conforms in some way to the themes and rhythms of the Book of Common Prayer, a dual focus on Word and Sacraments in their services, leadership by both clergy and laity, and usually an appreciation of what has often been called the Anglican *via media* or "middle way" (more on that later). But there are significant differences, as well, that have nothing to do with size.

High, Low, and In Between

Churches are first and foremost about worship, so *how* worship is done can be a very important factor to consider when looking for a spiritual home. As with the size of churches, there is a range of liturgical style to consider, but it can be narrowed down to a few key types.

First, there are *high churches*, sometimes called Anglo-Catholic because their style appears more Catholic than Protestant. These congregations value the use of all the senses in the worship experience. Indeed, this will be evident from the moment you walk through the doors, as you immediately notice the aroma of incense.

Drawing on a tradition as old as the ancient Hebrew people, incense is a symbol of the prayers of the people ascending to God. In a high church, incense is used in the liturgical procession in and out, and at various key moments in the service, such as when the Gospel is read or Eucharistic Prayer at the Altar. It is one of the reasons that high churches are sometimes affectionately called "smells and bells" churches.

Sight as well as smell is also tapped in a high church experience, as most evident in the procession. While almost all Episcopal churches make use of this parade-like entrance and exit by the liturgical party, a high church will usually offer greater numbers and varieties of participants in the procession, making for a grand spectacle. Your eyes will feast on a variety of colorful vestments with fascinating names. The priest might be wearing a flowing cape-like garment known as a cope, then when it is later time to stand at the Altar change into an overhead wrap called a chasuble. The deacon assisting at the Altar will likely be in another overhead wrap, similar to but noticeably different from a chasuble, known as a dalmatic. Acolytes, whether adults or young persons, will wear red or black cassocks covered by white surplices. And if a bishop is present and officiating, he or she will be wearing a mitre, the large, flame-shaped headgear, a symbol of the bishop's role as a successor to the apostles who on the day of Pentecost had "tongues of flame" descend upon them. The bishop will also undoubtedly carry a crozier, or shepherd's staff, a symbol of oversight as chief pastor over all the churches in his or her geographical diocese.

As for your hearing, not only will the choir take a lead in much of the worship, but the priest might very well chant, rather than say, the various prayers. The service also might well be in the poetic words and cadences of Elizabethan English ("It is meet and right so to do"), and some churches even utilize Latin for various hymns. Guests to a high church service often speak of a "reverent" quality to the service.

Then there are *low churches*, which in simplistic terms emphasize the Protestant tradition over the Catholic, or Word over Sacrament. These are churches where your hearing is key—the hearing of Scripture read and interpreted—and so the sermon is paramount and often longer than in higher churches. While a choir might still play an important role in both the procession and service, there is often a greater emphasis on congregational singing, and the variety of vestments is much more limited. Incense is rarely if ever used in a low church service, as again, the goal is to let nothing take attention away from the reading and preaching of God's Word.

Even clergy titles are different in high and low churches. In the former, the priest is likely to be called Father Jones or Mother Smith, while in the latter the priest is Reverend or Pastor or even Mr. Jones or Ms. Smith.

In the majority of churches somewhere on the continuum between extreme high and extreme low, there is a great deal of mixing different elements to fit the preferences and needs of the particular congregation and its clergy leaders. So, you will likely find priests in chasubles, but not switching in and out of copes or other vestments. You will likely find some chanting, such as with the psalm of the day, and maybe a few lines at the start of the Eucharistic Prayer, but nothing beyond that. You will likely not encounter incense (unless it is Christmas or Easter), and the sermon will be an important piece, but not longer than ten or twelve minutes. In other words, most places find worship patterns that work for their context.

And if a congregation has more than one service, as many do, then you can find a variety of worship even within that one church. The early service—starting at

8 a.m. or maybe 7:30 a.m.—is normally the quieter service, often without music, far smaller in size, intimate in nature. People often speak of the later service—perhaps at 10, 10:30, or 11 a.m.—as the main service, family service, or choir service. This is where you will find larger numbers of worshippers, the full procession down the main aisle, hymns and organ music, often a choir, and perhaps a longer sermon.

There might also be other types of services on Sunday or Saturday night, such as Celtic, Taizé, charismatic, contemporary, and jazz services, which offer alternative liturgical and musical styles, and thereby offer an even greater mix of possibilities.

With all this basic information, then, it is time to take the next step.

Do Some Detective Work

Some, like Mary, are invited to a church by a friend or co-worker and discover things when they arrive. But perhaps instead you decided on your own to look for a church, and that means doing some research. You might first go online, search for Episcopal churches in your area, and look at their websites. Check out their social media outlets. What do they say about themselves? What appear to be their priorities? How visitor-friendly do they appear to be at first glance? Practically, where are they and what times are their services? If you have kids, you might want to see if they have a nursery, children's program, youth program, etc. I often like to take an extra step and make a phone call to the parish office, asking a couple further questions. This not only helps me learn more, but also gives me the opportunity to connect with a human being and hear a verbal welcome.

So it's time to move from research to personal observation and experience. In other words, it's time to visit a church.

Hopefully the website, social media, or phone answering system made it clear how to find the church. I am always surprised (and dismayed) when I discover churches that seem to forget that visitors might not actually know how to get there! This needs to be made clear on the home page and on the answering machine message. And if parking is a problem or if there are specific instructions needed for parking, that needs to be clear as well. Most churches have designated handicapped parking spots. Some newcomer-friendly parishes have likewise introduced "first-time visitor" spots.

Upon parking, look for signs or indicators that make clear how to find the primary facilities you need: the church or sanctuary itself, the nursery, parish hall, youth room, parish office, and restrooms. Ask yourself some basic questions. Are the restrooms clean, fresh, and well lit? If you have children, would you be comfortable leaving them in the nursery? Many churches use a check-in system, so that you leave your cell number with the nursery worker in case there is an emergency while you are in the worship service. And whether it is the nursery or a youth room, it is important to note the furniture. Too often have some churches allowed well-intentioned members to donate used sofas, chairs, toys, and other items that are old and worn out. Make sure that the places you visit don't skimp on things that matter. New, fresh items are worth the investment.

The goal in all this is to help interested newcomers not only find their way to the church, but also feel welcome and comfortable once they arrive. Some wise vestries—the board of laypersons who work with the clergy in overseeing the congregation—actually take "field trips" or their own property and even enlist the help of "mystery church shoppers" to assist them in seeing their church and its systems through the eyes of a newcomer. Such actions show remarkable care.

And then, of course, there is the personal touch. What are the people like? Most churches have ushers, who greet you when you enter the sanctuary, hand you a worship program, and direct you to open seats. Some other churches have gone the extra mile and created what might be called an "ambassador" program, with interested members trained to do more than say hello. They see themselves as the first wave of radical welcome, and might even host a table in front of the church doors, offering material about the parish and answering questions you might have.

If the service itself is a positive experience (and we will talk about what to expect in the service in Chapter 3), then you might want to join others in the coffee hour that follows or is between services. This is a wonderful opportunity to encounter not just the "ambassadors" but the regular folks who comprise the congregation. If you are an extrovert, this can simply add to the good energy. But if that sounds intimidating or just plain exhausting, if you have little desire to interact on your first visit, then at least consider filling in the "first-time visitor" card that undoubtedly is in the pew or chair. Don't worry, they won't bombard you with calls or emails, but it does allow the church leaders to know you were there, pray for you, and be on the lookout when you return. It is a nice way to connect without interacting right then.

Research, observation, detective work . . . it all sounds like work. But the fact is that choosing a church that can become your spiritual home is worth the effort.

What Do I Do When I'm There?

"Accept us now, as we dedicate this place to which we come to praise your Name, to ask your forgiveness, to know your healing power, to hear your Word, and to be nourished by the Body and Blood of your Son." (BCP, p. 568)

As already noted, at its heart, church is about worship. So perhaps it is time to get acquainted more closely with what goes on in the service. As noted already, it all starts with the *procession*. Far from being a simple parade, the procession is a reminder of the people of God in every generation "pressing on toward the goal," as the apostle Paul so beautifully describes it. We stand and sing our song of praise as the clergy and the others in the liturgical party, representing all of us, move forward from the west end of the church toward the rising of the sun, toward the sanctuary even as the High Priest thousands of years ago processed through the temple into the Holy of Holies. The procession is about all of us moving "from grace to grace," never stagnant, always following the call of Christ ever onward, ever onward.

Following the procession, the celebrant (either the bishop, if present, or more commonly the priest) opens with a word of welcome and blessing, and with the aptly-named *Collect of Purity*, with which we acknowledge from the start that the God whom we worship is the One "to whom all hearts are open, all desires known, and from whom no secrets are hid."

It is small wonder that we follow up immediately with either the *Gloria in Excelsis* or the *Kyrie*, depending on the season of the church year in which we find ourselves. With the Gloria, we burst out into the hymn of praise once sung by the angels at Jesus's birth. With the Kyrie, we cry out "Lord, have mercy . . . Christ, have mercy." It is all about recognizing the Good News that God is God, so we don't have to try to be. To praise God, to acknowledge the divine, is to let go of some of our own need to be all and do all. As Paul said to the Corinthian Christians, "We do not proclaim ourselves, but Jesus Christ as Lord, and ourselves as your servants for Jesus's sake." Before sitting down to hear the readings from Scripture, the celebrant prays the *Collect of the Day*, which collects the thoughts of the biblical passages we will hear into a focused prayer.

Already we can see a kinetic pattern emerging: we stand to sing and praise, we sit to receive instruction, and we kneel to confess our sins and, for some, to pray. Stand, sit, and kneel. Different churches might do some of it slightly differently, but the basic pattern remains.

And so we move into the *Liturgy of the Word*, which includes an Old Testament reading, a psalm, a New Testament epistle, a gospel reading, and the sermon. People are sometimes surprised when they find out how much Scripture is part of our Episcopal worship. And the passages read are not chosen simply at the whim of the preacher but rather are part of the church's lectionary, which works through the Bible in a three-year cycle. Note that people sit for the other readings, but stand for the reading of the Gospel, which is done by a deacon if present.

After the sermon, the people stand and together recite the centuries-old *Nicene Creed*, a summary of our Christian faith. You may notice some people making the sign of the cross at the end of the Creed. This is personal preference, but for many, it is a way of sealing what that person has just professed, a kind of non-verbal "Amen." The Creed is followed by the *Prayers of the People*, led by either a deacon or a layperson.

These prayers might be slightly different in their specifics each week, but they always follow a pattern of praying for the church, the nation, the poor, the sick, and the faithful departed. After the prayers, the people kneel and join in the *General Confession* and *Absolution.* This opportunity to admit that we have sinned and are in need of forgiveness is a response to all that has come before in the hearing of Holy Scripture and preparation for coming to Holy Communion. It is a cleansing, a fresh start, done together.

How appropriate, then, that the first half of the service concludes with *The Peace,* when a people who have listened to God's Word, proclaimed their faith, prayed for the world, and confessed their own failings now embrace one another as a people loved, absolved, and renewed. Although some do embrace one another as they share the Peace, many others shake hands. In most churches, the people then sit as various announcements are shared, newcomers are formally welcomed, and persons celebrating their birthdays or anniversaries are called forward and blessed.

The bridge between the first and second halves of the service is *The Offertory,* when the people "pass the plate" and give financially for the ongoing mission and ministry. Often, this occurs while the choir sings an anthem. This is something more than paying your dues to be part of the club, and it is far more than a handout to the church. We give to God through the church out of gratitude. We give because we recognize that all we have is gift. So the priest says when receiving the people's offerings, "All things come of you, O God." And the people stand and reply, "And of your own have we given you."

Do note that while the people's gifts were being received, the Altar, sometimes referred to as the Holy Table, was prepared for what follows. The setting of the Altar is done by a deacon, if present, and otherwise by the priest. With this done, we move from the Liturgy of the Word to the *Liturgy of the Sacrament*, as the celebrant and all the people stand for the Eucharistic Prayer. Between the Book of Common Prayer and other Church-authorized supplemental texts such as *Enriching our Worship*, our Episcopal tradition has several options to use for the Eucharistic Prayer. Some fit better in certain seasons of the church year, such as Advent or Lent, while others are more intentional in using gender-inclusive language. But they all contain a recital of salvation history, culminating in the words that Jesus himself said at the Last Supper, "This is my Body, this is my Blood."

While most people in the congregation follow the celebrant's lead and remain standing throughout the Eucharistic Prayer, you just might see some kneel instead, as a sign of their personal piety. As with crossing one's self at the end of the creed, there is no right or wrong answer to whether you stand or kneel in the Eucharistic Prayer. It is your personal preference. But all are called boldly to say "Amen!" at the end of the lengthy prayer, and then all in their respective languages are called to pray together *the Lord's Prayer*.

This is followed by *the Fraction*, when the celebrant breaks the bread and invites the congregation to receive both it and the cup of wine, now the consecrated body and blood of Christ. Note that "Alleluia" is said here (and in other parts of the service) in all seasons of the church year except during Lent.

The people are invited to go forward at *the Communion* with hands open and palms up to receive the bread and then drink the wine. If for any reason you are not comfortable receiving either the bread or wine or both, simply go forward with your arms folded across your chest, and the clergy will give you a blessing. Either way, you can return to your seat and either sit or kneel as hymns or music continues.

After the entire congregation has had the opportunity to receive, the Altar is cleared and the celebrant leads the people in one last *Post-Communion Prayer*, followed immediately by the final *Blessing*, given at the Altar by the bishop or priest. Some will kneel for this, though most will likely remain standing. The deacon, if present, offers the words of the *Dismissal*, which call on all of us to go and be God's faithful ambassadors in our homes, our neighborhoods, and our workplaces. Our service of worship has ended; now the service of our lives and witness for Christ begins.

Throughout this service, you have been more than a spectator; you have participated in this divine drama, even as faithful followers of Christ have done so throughout time and throughout the world. It is perfectly fine if you didn't quite know what to do at certain points. Just dive in where you are comfortable and don't worry about the rest. As you return, you will find that soon the words and actions (stand-sit-kneel) become more familiar, and eventually second nature. What is important is for you to let go of any nervousness you might have and simply join in.

As with our friend Mary at the start, you can find all kinds of ways to become more fully involved with the church. There is usually some kind of newcomers' or inquirers' class that is led over several weeks by either the priest or a lay leader. This is a great opportunity to learn the basics about the parish. There also are often congregational events, dinners, prayer circles, and study groups where you can get to know people and experience the life of the congregation. The church probably has opportunities for volunteer service, as well, which can take various forms such as food pantries, Habitat building projects, and outreach to schools and nursing homes. And there are many opportunities at the church to lend a hand and make a difference, whether it is helping in the altar guild, teaching Sunday school, or singing in the choir. And, of course, you can make an appointment with the clergy or other church leaders just to have some one-on-one time and ask whatever you want.

The Episcopal Church Welcomes You

It's true that you don't have to go to church to encounter God. But why not dare to discover what so many others throughout the years and across the globe have found: that being part of a community of people like you, imperfect but beloved, can bring fresh meaning and peace to your own life.

In the first century, the earliest followers of Jesus devoted themselves, as the New Testament book of Acts says, "to the apostles' teaching and fellowship, to the breaking of bread and the prayers." It wasn't long before tensions emerged within the community. That is no surprise, as those early churches included people of different backgrounds, traditions, and ideas. But as both the book of Acts and the letters of the apostle Paul go on to show, those first Christians worked on their life together, because they knew that their life together was worth it. For together, despite their imperfections and idiosyncrasies, they became a force for good that changed the world. And each of them was changed in the process.

In the twenty-first century, people in urban centers, suburban neighborhoods, and rural byways catch a glimpse of a familiar road sign that declares, "The Episcopal Church Welcomes You." Accompanying these words is the name of a nearby church and its location. Also on the sign is the Episcopal shield, our family coat of arms, as it were. It is comprised of the St. George's cross and the St. Andrew's cross, a tribute to our two mother churches, the Church of England and the Scottish Episcopal Church. It is a rich heritage that welcomes you. It is a life-affirming tradition that welcomes you. It is a local community with global connections that welcomes you. The welcome sign is an extended hand. It is up to you to take it and see what comes.

As you walk through the doors of your local church, who knows where those steps will lead. You might just find that you have embarked on a journey that takes you deeper into a community of faith and love, and ultimately into the heart of God.

For Further Exploration

If you would like to dig deeper and explore more about our Episcopal liturgy, history, and tradition, then feel free to dive into any of these books. You might also want to visit the church's official website at www.episcopalchurch.org.

Black, Vicki. *Welcome to the Book of Common Prayer* (Church Publishing, 2005). This is a helpful how-to introduction to the prayer book.

Freeman, Len, et al. *Ashes and the Phoenix: Meditations for the Season of Lent* (Forward Movement, 2016). This is a poetic window into the spiritual life, and an excellent way to develop your own Lenten discipline.

Kitch, Anne E. *Preparing for Baptism in the Episcopal Church* (Church Publishing, 2015). This is an accessible resource for adults who want to be baptized and parents who seek to baptize their infants or children.

Markham, Ian. *Faith Rules: An Episcopal Manual* (Church Publishing, 2016). This is a beautifully illustrated guide to the Christian faith and the Episcopal Church.

Markham, Ian and Robertson, C. K. *Episcopal Questions, Episcopal Answers* (Morehouse Publishing, 2014). This is a clear and concise Q&A introduction to the church, addressing foundational questions of faith and church practice.

Pritchard, Robert W. *A History of the Episcopal Church, 3rd rev. ed. Through the 78th General Convention* (Morehouse Publishing, 2014). This is an updated version of a popular volume that runs from the Episcopal Church's beginnings to 2014.

Robertson, C. K. *The Book of Common Prayer: A Spiritual Treasure Chest* (SkyLight Paths/Turner Publishing, 2013). This contains selected passages from the prayer book with facing-page commentary that makes the text relevant for today.

Robertson, C. K. *Transforming Stewardship* (Church Publishing, 2009). This is a practical approach to congregational life and being "stewards of others."

The Path: A Journey through the Bible (Forward Movement, 2016). This is a great tool for familiarizing yourself with the Bible.

Ware, Jordan Haynie. *The Ultimate Quest: A Geek's Guide to (The Episcopal) Church* (Church Publishing, 2017). This is a humorous introduction to the Episcopal Church in language that young adults and geeks of all ages will understand and appreciate.

Yaw, Chris. *Jesus Was an Episcopalian (and You Can be One Too!): A Newcomer's Guide to the Episcopal Church* (Leader Resources, 2008). This is an engaging book for newcomers and returnees alike to take a look at the Church.

Episcopal Terminology

I often remind congregational leaders that we too often use insider language, or as the apostle Paul put it in his first letter to the Corinthian Christians, we "speak in tongues." In 1 Corinthians 14, Paul urged that if "tongues" are used in a church, then someone should be ready to interpret them. There are various online glossaries available, but for now you might find the following helpful.

Church Architecture

Apse
: A semicircular vaulted area within the chancel of some cathedrals or churches, usually where the Altar stands or the clergy are seated.

Chancel
: Also known as the sanctuary, the area at the front (east) end of the church, containing the Altar, pulpit, and seats for officiating ministers, usually raised slightly above the nave.

Narthex   The vestibule, or first section of the church, when you walk in from the main (west) entryway.

Nave   The central part of the church, from the narthex to the chancel, where the people are seated during the service.

Sacristy   The area in the church, unseen by most, where the various accoutrements for the service are stored, prepared, and cleaned, and where the clergy and lay ministers vest themselves.

Sanctuary   The chancel, though the word is sometimes used to speak of the entire church building, as distinct from other facilities on the church campus.

Church Roles

Acolyte   Either an adult or a young person, this person assists the officiating ministers, sometimes carrying the cross (then referred to as the crucifer), or a large candle (a torchbearer), or the censer with incense (a thurifer), or fulfilling other duties as necessary.

Bishop   Overseer and chief pastor of a diocese, the geographical region containing multiple church congregations. Often noticeable by a purple clerical shirt, and in a liturgical setting by wearing the hat

	known as a mitre and carrying the crozier, or shepherd's staff.
Celebrant	The bishop or priest who officiates over a Eucharistic service, also known as the presider.
Deacon	A person called and ordained primarily to the ministry of service, directly accountable to the bishop, and bringing the needs of the world to the church.
Laity	One of the four Orders of Ministry, lay persons are not ordained but are called in their Baptismal Covenant to proclaim Christ by word and action in all areas of their lives.
Presiding Bishop	Chief Pastor and Primate of The Episcopal Church, elected by the House of Bishops and confirmed by the House of Deputies at the General Convention to serve a nine-year term.
Priest	The term being a contraction of the word "presbyter," it refers to a person called and ordained primarily to serve as pastor to the people, offering blessing and absolution, administering the Sacraments and preaching the gospel, and working with the bishop in the administration of the church.
Priest-in-Charge	A priest working full or part-time with a contract by the annual appointment of

the bishop, responsible for liturgy, preaching and teaching, pastoral care, and administration as negotiated with the vestry.

Rector

A full-time priest elected by the vestry and approved by the bishop, thereby having tenure.

Sexton

A person, usually working part or full-time, charged with taking care of the church facilities.

Verger

A lay person who acts behind the scenes in the logistical preparation and implementation of worship services and who then vests and leads the procession, carrying the traditional "virge," a staff which in older times might have been used to keep back overenthusiastic crowds.

Vestry

The governing board of the local parish, consisting of lay persons elected to the office for a term, usually three years, and primarily responsible for property, finances, and the calling of a new rector.

Vicar

A priest, full or part-time, responsible for an aided or mission congregation, one that is not self-supporting like a parish. While a vicar has most of the responsibilities of a rector, this person does not have tenure but is appointed by the bishop for a period of time.

Church Seasons

Advent
: From a Latin word meaning "coming," this first season of the church year begins four Sundays before Christmas and emphasizes anticipation and preparation for the coming of Jesus. The liturgical color used in Advent is either light blue (representing Mary) or purple (for penitence).

All Saints
: Also known as All Hallows Day, this feast is held on November 1, commemorates all God's saints, both living and dead, and is a reminder of the bond we have in Christ with those who have already passed on into the larger Life. The color for All Saints is white.

Ascension
: The Thursday forty days after the Feast of the Resurrection, or Easter, when we commemorate the risen Jesus ascending to heaven. The color for Ascension Thursday is white.

Christmas
: The Feast of the Nativity, held on December 25, commemorating the birth of Jesus. Though most people think of Christmas Day only, it is the first day in a twelve-day season culminating with the Feast of the Epiphany. The color for Christmas is white.

Easter
: The Feast of the Resurrection, a moveable feast with no fixed date like Christmas or All Saints. Celebrated on the first Sunday

after the full moon following the spring equinox, a formula for determining the date in any given year is found in the back section of the Book of Common Prayer. The Prayer Book also includes a special service called the Great Vigil of Easter, to be held after sunset on Saturday. The color for Easter is white.

Epiphany

January 6, ending the Twelve Days of Christmas, and commemorating the coming of the Wise Men to the baby Jesus. The Season of Epiphany lasts until Ash Wednesday. The First Sunday of Epiphany is traditionally associated with the baptism of Jesus and therefore a principal day (along with Easter Eve, Pentecost, and All Saints) for Christian baptisms. The color for Epiphany is white.

Lent

From an Anglo-Saxon word meaning "spring," Lent is a forty-day period of intentional self-examination and penitence beginning with Ash Wednesday and culminating with Holy Week, with services for Palm Sunday, Maundy Thursday, Good Friday, and Holy Saturday found in the Book of Common Prayer. Churches often use this season to host simple suppers and mid-week teachings or home studies. The color for Lent is purple.

Pentecost

Literally "the fiftieth day" after Easter, commemorating the coming of the Holy Spirit on the first disciples as they were celebrating the Jewish Feast of Shavuot or "Weeks." The key reading this day comes from the Acts of the Apostles and is often read in different languages, a reminder of how people of various tongues heard Peter and the apostles preaching as if in their own language, with three thousand new converts added to their number. The color of Pentecost is red, and the color of the Sundays in the season after Pentecost is green.

Church Services

Baptism

As the Book of Common Prayer succinctly puts it, Holy Baptism is "full initiation by water and the Holy Spirit into Christ's Body, the Church."

Compline

The final service of the day, which may be officiated by a member of either the clergy or laity. The service may be used either in church or at home.

Confirmation

A service that seals the covenant made at baptism, in which those who are "ready and have been duly prepared to make a mature public affirmation of their faith and commitment to the responsibilities of their baptism" do so in the presence of the bishop, who then lays hands on their head and prays that God will strengthen them and empower them for God's service. Preparation is usually in the form of confirmation classes at the local parish.

Evensong

Also known as "vespers," this service occurs around sunset and often involves a choir chanting the various parts. When said instead of sung, the service is called Evening Prayer.

Matins

Also known as Morning Prayer, this service is also part of the Daily Office in the prayer book, and at times is used in some churches in place of the Eucharist. The officiant may be a lay person.

Rite I and II

These terms refer to the types of liturgies found in the Book of Common Prayer that can be used for Eucharist, Morning and Evening Prayer, Burial, and so forth. More specifically, Rite I uses the Elizabethan English and liturgical expressions, such as "And with thy spirit" or "It is meet and right so to do" as contrasted with the modern American English and liturgical expressions, such as "And also with you" or "It is right to give thanks and praise." With the new authorized supplement to the prayer book, *Enriching Our Worship,* congregations have even more inclusive language and liturgical styles from which to choose.

Church Vestments

Alb
: The basic white, full-length garment worn in a liturgy, sometimes with just a stole and sometimes under a chasuble. It is like the tunics worn by the ancient Romans.

Cassock
: Literally "long coat," this ankle-length garment, black for priests and purple for bishops, used to be the common everyday attire for clergy, but now is used mainly in liturgical settings, underneath other vestments.

Chasuble
: Literally "little house," this poncho-like outer garment is worn by priests and bishops at the Eucharist. There are different colored chasubles for the various church seasons.

Chimere
: Worn by bishops over a rochet, it resembles an academic gown, but without sleeves.

Cincture
: The rope or band worn at the waist over an alb or cassock.

Cope
: Literally "cape," a liturgical cloak worn over the alb, open in the front and fastened at the breast with a band, and worn in processions by any member of the

	clergy. When used by a bishop, it is accompanied by a mitre.
Mitre	Literally "headband," this traditional headgear worn by bishops resembles a flame, with two short lappets hanging down from the back. It is reminiscent of the tongues of flame that descended on the heads of the apostles with the coming of the Holy Spirit on Pentecost.
Rochet	A version of the alb worn by bishops when not serving at the Altar.
Stole	A long, narrow strip of fabric, worn hanging down from the neck like a scarf by a priest or bishop in Eucharistic settings, and across the chest and back with the ends connected together on one side by a deacon. There are different colored stoles for the various church seasons.
Surplice	A shortened version of the alb, worn over a surplice in non-Eucharistic service such as Morning or Evening Prayer.
Tippet	Also known as a "preaching scarf," this long, black ceremonial scarf is worn in non-Eucharistic settings (such as Morning or Evening Prayer) by a priest.